GODS OF INDIA

Narsimha Saves Prahlad

SHUBHA VILAS

Lord Vishnu is hailed as the preserver and sustainer of the Universe. One of the holy trinity of Hindu gods, Vishnu has appeared nine times as an avatar to rid the Earth from evil, and to empower the good, and thereby restore Dharma in order to maintain cosmic harmony.

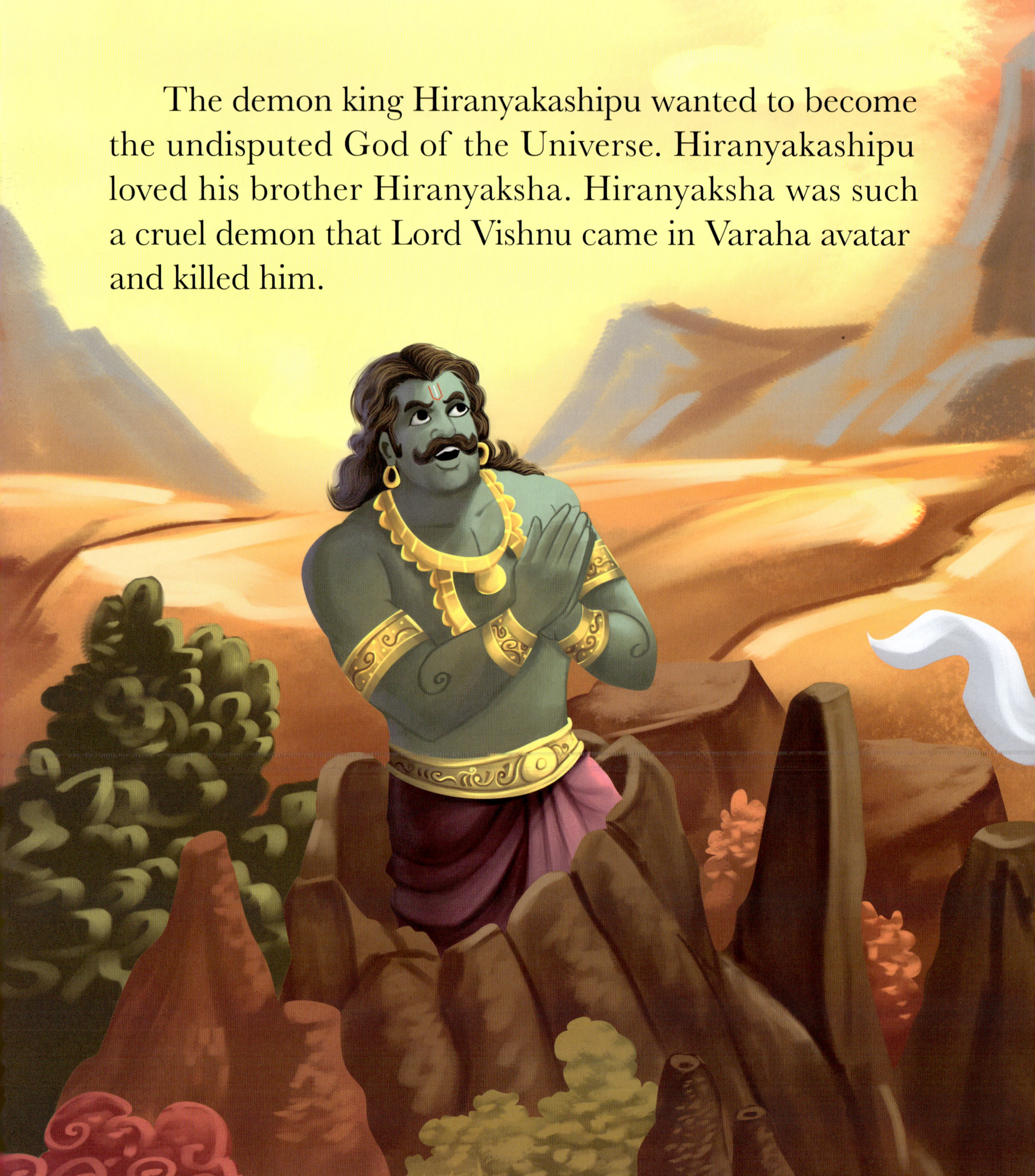

The demon king Hiranyakashipu wanted to become the undisputed God of the Universe. Hiranyakashipu loved his brother Hiranyaksha. Hiranyaksha was such a cruel demon that Lord Vishnu came in Varaha avatar and killed him.

Hiranyakashipu, when he heard the bad news, went mad with rage. With revenge on his mind, Hiranyakashipu did severe austerities for thousands of years to please Lord Brahma and eventually obtained a boon from him that made him invincible. He could not be killed on Earth nor space. Not by fire nor by water; neither during day nor at night; neither inside nor outside (of a home); nor by a human, animal or god; nor by any weapon. With a boon like this, the demon king unleashed terror and ordered his soldiers to kill anyone who was found worshipping Vishnu.

Hiranyakashipu's son Prahlad was born to Kayadhu (Hiranyakashipu's wife), while the demon king was in the Himalayas doing intense penance to please Lord Brahma for obtaining a boon.

Prahlad was destined to take birth at the humble abode of Devarshi Narad Muni, and none other than Goddess Yogmaya helped Kayadhu deliver her baby. Prahlad had the blessings of Lord Vishnu and the gods even when he was in his mother's womb.

Prahlad was one of the greatest devotees of Lord Vishnu. He was the disciple of Narada Muni and had started chanting the name of Lord Vishnu while he was in his mother's womb.

Hence, despite being the son of an asura, Prahlad exhibited divine qualities. Among the many of those who opposed the cruel king was his own flesh and blood, Prahlad. Imagine the wicked Hiranyakashipu's anger when he learnt about his son's devotion to Vishnu. He attempted to dissuade him. But when he failed to do so, he laid several traps to kill him.

When Prahlad repeatedly defied his father and insisted on following ways of a devotee rather than a demon, his father tried to kill him. He sent his servants to attack Prahlad with weapons. He threw him in front of mad elephants. Locked him up with venomous snakes. Flung him down a huge mountain.

But would you believe it…every time, Prahlad was miraculously saved by divine powers. Not a hair on his head was hurt.

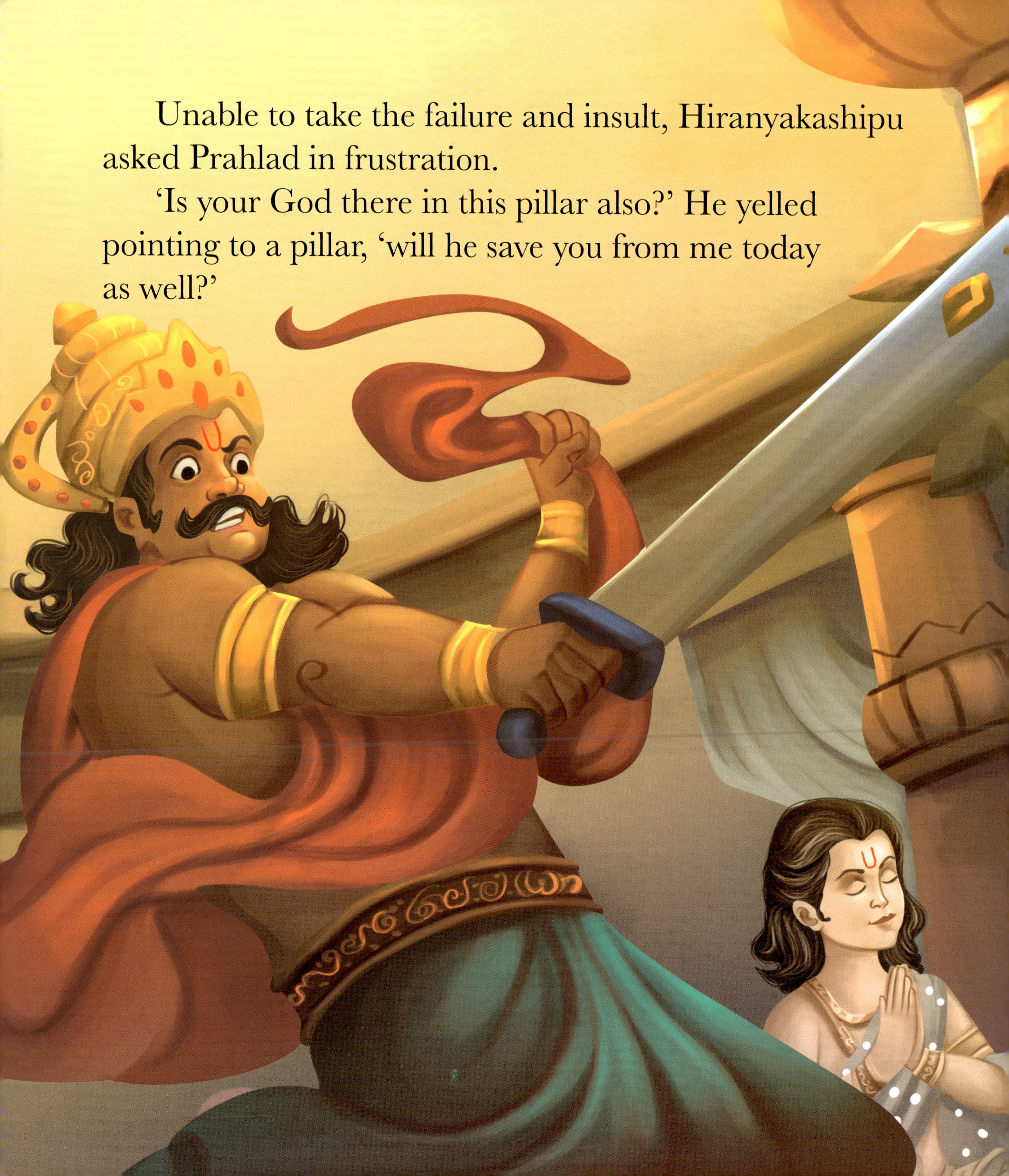

Unable to take the failure and insult, Hiranyakashipu asked Prahlad in frustration.

'Is your God there in this pillar also?' He yelled pointing to a pillar, 'will he save you from me today as well?'

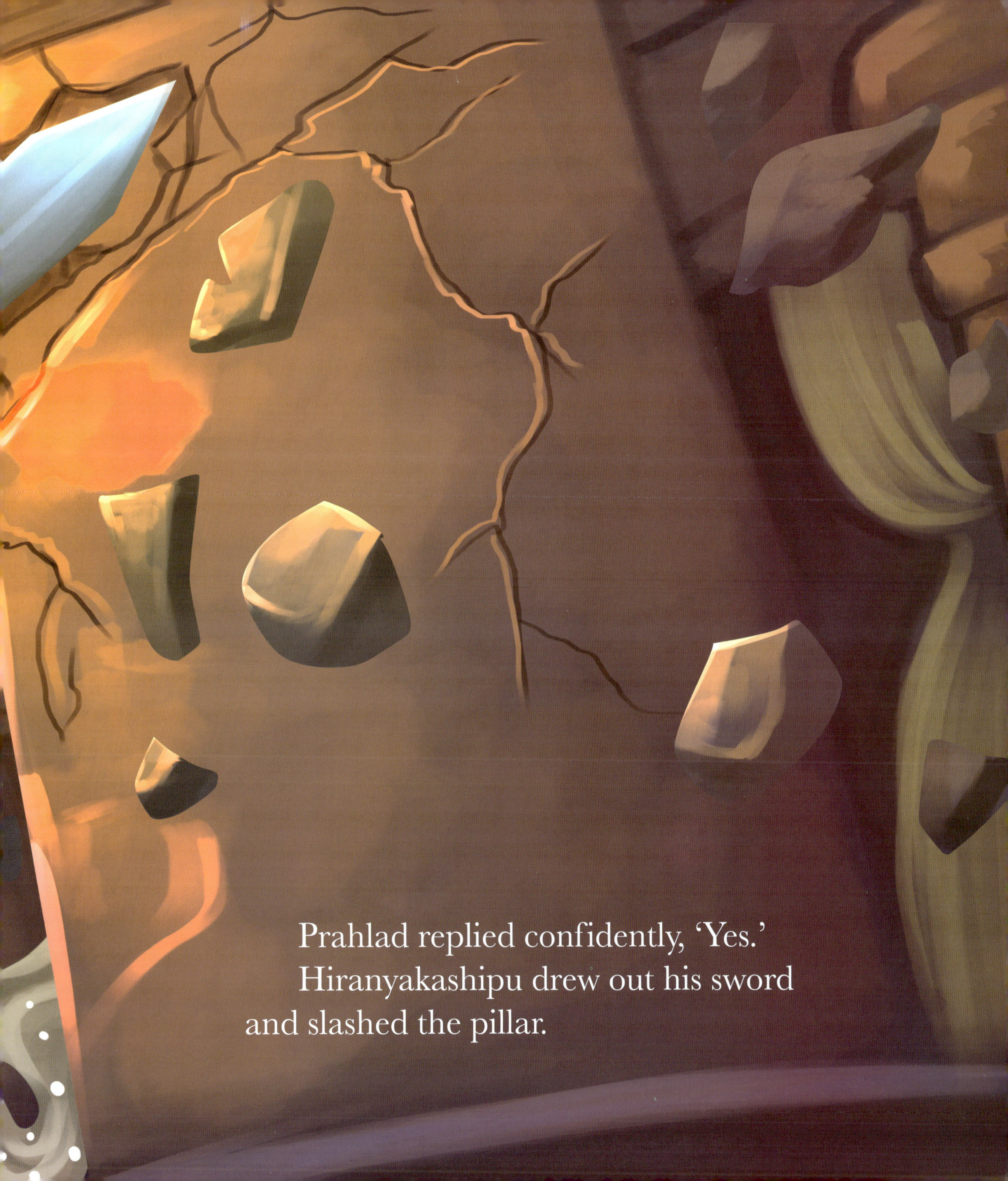

Prahlad replied confidently, 'Yes.'

Hiranyakashipu drew out his sword and slashed the pillar.

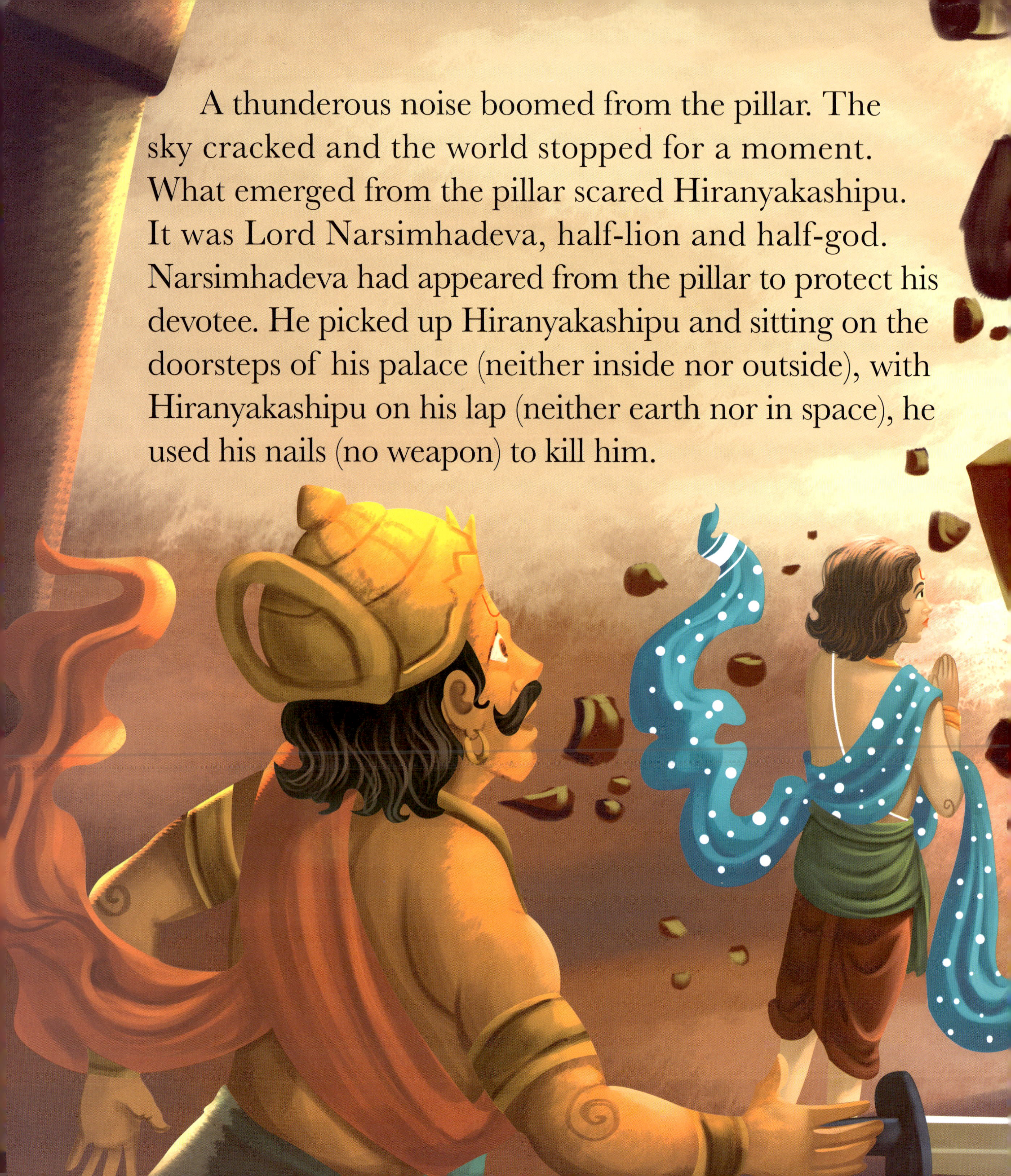

A thunderous noise boomed from the pillar. The sky cracked and the world stopped for a moment. What emerged from the pillar scared Hiranyakashipu. It was Lord Narsimhadeva, half-lion and half-god. Narsimhadeva had appeared from the pillar to protect his devotee. He picked up Hiranyakashipu and sitting on the doorsteps of his palace (neither inside nor outside), with Hiranyakashipu on his lap (neither earth nor in space), he used his nails (no weapon) to kill him.

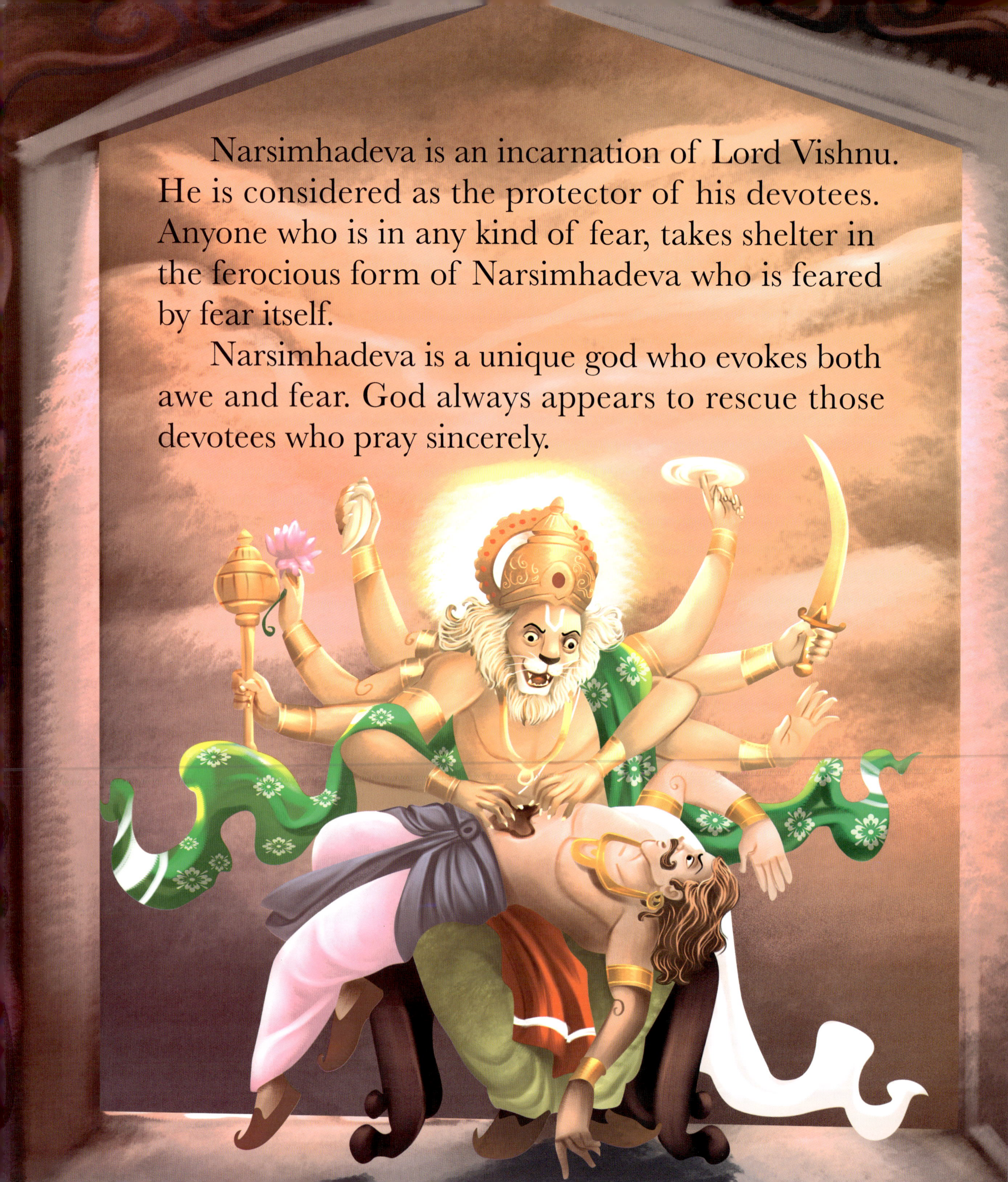

Narsimhadeva is an incarnation of Lord Vishnu. He is considered as the protector of his devotees. Anyone who is in any kind of fear, takes shelter in the ferocious form of Narsimhadeva who is feared by fear itself.

Narsimhadeva is a unique god who evokes both awe and fear. God always appears to rescue those devotees who pray sincerely.